P9-DDL-961

Olivia's Birds
Saving the Gulf

by Olivia Bouler

This book belongs to:

Audubon

Olivia's Birds
Saving the Gulf

by Olivia Bouler

STERLING CHILDREN'S BOOKS
New York

This book is dedicated to my little brother Jackson whose love helped my dreams take flight.

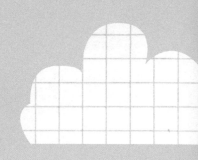

STERLING and the distinctive Sterling logo are registered trademarks of Sterling Publishing Co., Inc.

Library of Congress Cataloging-in-Publication Data
Bouler, Olivia.
Olivia's birds : saving the Gulf / by Olivia Bouler.
    p. cm.
  ISBN 978-1-4027-8665-5
  1. Birds--Juvenile literature. 2. Nature conservation--Juvenile literature. I. Title.
  QL676.2.B677 2011
  598--dc22   2010046002

Lot#:
10 9 8 7 6 5 4 3 2 1
01/11
Published by Sterling Publishing Co., Inc.
387 Park Avenue South, New York, NY 10016
Text and illustrations © 2011 by Olivia Bouler
Distributed in Canada by Sterling Publishing
C/o Canadian Manda Group, 165 Dufferin Street
Toronto, Ontario, Canada M6K 3H6
Distributed in the United Kingdom by GMC Distribution Services
Castle Place, 166 High Street, Lewes, East Sussex, England BN7 1XU
Distributed in Australia by Capricorn Link (Australia) Pty. Ltd.
P.O. Box 704, Windsor, NSW 2756, Australia

Printed in China

Sterling ISBN 978-1-4027-8665-5

For information about custom editions, special sales, premium and corporate purchases, please contact Sterling Special Sales Department at 800-805-5489 or specialsales@sterlingpublishing.com.

Photos by James Bouler
Photo on p. 5 by Bill Scholtz
Photo on p. 26 © Steve Nesius/Disney Channel
Designed by Merideth Harte

The Audubon mission is to conserve and restore natural ecosystems, focusing on birds, other wildlife, and their habitats for the benefit of humanity and the earth's biological diversity. To learn how you can support Audubon, call (800) 274-4201, visit www.audubon.org, or write to Audubon, 225 Varick St., 7th Flr, New York, New York, 10014.

Dr. Steve Kress
Director,
Project Puffin

Project Puffin
SEABIRD RESTORATION PROGRAM
DEDICATED TO SEABIRD CONSERVATION

Audubon
www.projectpuffin.org
www.audubon.org
Email: puffin@audubon.org

159 Sapsucker Woods Road • Ithaca, New York 14850 USA
Tel: (607) 257-7308 • FAX: (607) 257-6231

12 Audubon Road • Bremen, Maine 04551 USA
Tel: (207) 529-5828 • FAX: (207) 529-5688

I met Olivia Bouler at the Project Puffin Visitor Center in Rockland, Maine. I was curious about this 11-year-old bird artist, as I too had sketched birds at her age, which led me to a career helping birds. Olivia is unusually perceptive, both as a person and as an artist. Her ability to see a bird in her mind's eye and then capture its form with line and color is well matched with her unique ornithological perspective.

Through our own independent good fortunes, Olivia and I have both come to the same conclusion—that good intentions are not enough. Project Puffin has shown me that action in the face of huge obstacles is the only way to make a real contribution, and this is Olivia's message as well. People of any age can make a difference. They just need a good idea and the persistence to see it through.

Inside this book, you'll find Olivia's "If I Were President" platform, which includes simple, do-able ideas for people of all ages. Should the happy day come when Olivia actually does run for president, she has my vote!

Dr. Steve Kress
Director, Project Puffin

Discovering Birds

Common Nighthawk
This bird nests on roofs and is often mistaken for a swallow at night.

Birds are fascinating, intriguing, and unique creatures.

Some birds are colorful and pretty to look at. Other birds, like the chickadee, are so friendly that they will eat right out of your hand.

There are lots of different types of birds. Some are all around you—in trees, on the tops of telephone poles, and even on your roof!

Osprey
The osprey builds huge nests, high off the ground.

Everyday Birds

Blue Jay
Blue Jays can imitate the calls of various eagles and hawks.

Northern Cardinal
Males with brighter feathers feed more food to their young!

American Goldfinch
Its nickname is "wild canary" due to its bright yellow plumage.

You may not notice the birds around you, but there are lots of them right outside your window! You don't have to travel anywhere to look for them.

For example, the graceful Barn Swallow lives in the crevices of buildings and on the sides of schools. They can usually be found "dancing" in soccer fields or meadows.

If you take a look around, you might catch a glimpse of a White Breasted Nuthatch climbing a tree upside-down!

Which birds do you see outside **your** window?

Vulture

Birds in Flight

Did you know that birds learn how to fly from their parents? Bird parents will nudge the babies off the nest. The chicks will either fall or fly out of the tree. If they fall, the parents will swoop them back up until they learn how to fly!

Some birds can't fly, like penguins and the Kiwi from New Zealand. But most birds are amazing flyers.

Songbirds fly in a flutter pattern. They flutter and then close their wings before fluttering again. Vultures fly in circles looking for prey. Ducks and waterfowl flap their wings very hard and never take a break. Their way of flying looks like it hurts!

There is no other animal equipped just like birds. Even the bat can't fly as well or aerodynamically as a bird can. Birds are flying elegance.

Barred Owl
Owls flap to take off and glide silently so their prey doesn't detect them.

The Canada Goose
Geese flap constantly until they are ready to land in water. Their webbed feet break their fall.

Warbler

Birds That Live in the Woods

Black-billed Magpie
This bird is a relative of crows and jays.

M ost birds live in trees—and where are there lots of trees? In woods and forests!

Some of the best bird watching can be done in a forest, far away from civilization. If you sit still, birds will certainly come out of hiding. Be sure to bring your binoculars and a camera. And don't just look up. I once found a hummingbird nest on the ground of a wooded area.

Tufted Titmouse
This small, fuzzy friend is shy but will visit frequently if it finds food in your yard.

Thrum... WHUMP WHACK!

Pileated Woodpecker
"Thrum... WHUMP WHACK!" The Pileated Woodpecker's familiar tree-pecking drum is often mistaken for the Ivory-billed Woodpecker.

13

Birds That Live Near Water

Razorbill
These unique birds can chase prey underwater as deep as 400 feet!

Imagine yourself sitting in a boat, listening to the pouring rush of water as it moves gently downstream. Doesn't that sound nice? Well, some birds think it's nice, too!

Many birds live near lakes, streams, and oceans. They need to nest there in order to survive. It takes over a thousand years for coastal birds to adapt to a new environment! That's a really long time.

Atlantic Puffin
This cute but hardy bird was once nearly extinct off the coast of Maine.

Roseate Spoonbill
Their spoon-shaped bills filter food, and the chemicals in its diet turn it pink!

Hummingbird

Weird & Wacky Birds

 **S**ome birds do the most interesting, unusual things. Whether it's their curious call, or the strange shape of their bill, or perhaps their unique role in our environment, some birds don't seem like birds at all.

Eastern Phoebe
Dogs wag their tails—and so do these birds perched on a branch!

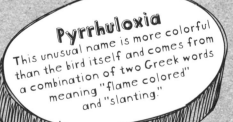

Pyrrhuloxia
This unusual name is more colorful than the bird itself and comes from a combination of two Greek words meaning "flame colored" and "slanting."

Scissor-tailed Flycatcher
Its name says it all! This bird eats flies and other small insects. When it crosses its tail, it looks like a pair of scissors.

Bald Eagle

Fierce Birds

Cooper's Hawk
This bird was nicknamed "chicken hawk" because it liked to hunt chickens on farms.

American Kestrel
This robin-sized bird may be small, but it is fierce enough to take on bats, birds, and even fish.

What do you think of first when you hear "birds of prey?" Feisty falcons clutching their lunch in their sharp talons? Or perhaps what comes to mind is our nation's bird, the Bald Eagle, standing proudly with our flag?

Some birds are hunters and can be very aggressive. That's just their nature. They need to eat and live, too!

If you want to watch these birds, it's best to stay 20 feet away and use a scope or a pair of binoculars. If you happen to find yourself near one of their nests, don't panic! Put your hands down by your side and back away slowly.

Swallow-tailed Kite
Agile, aerodynamic, and often called the most beautiful bird in America, Swallow-tailed Kites shoot out of the sky to pounce on unsuspecting prey.

1   2   3   4

Four Stages of Development

Bird Beauty

Lazuli Bunting
With a striking blue nape, vibrant orange chest, and white underbelly, this bird has amazing variation in its color.

id you know that all baby birds are born kind of naked? It's true!

Birds develop in four stages. In the first stage, chicks have very dark feathers that are used for camouflage and warmth. They grow head feathers, chest feathers, and their first wing feathers in the second stage. In the third stage of development, birds grow more wing feathers and tail feathers for balance. By the fourth stage, birds have grown their flight feathers and are ready to take to the skies.

You can tell a lot about an adult bird by its feathers. Male birds are more colorful than females. They use their feathers for showing off and attracting mates.

Female birds have duller feathers that act like camouflage. The mother birds guard the nest and protect their chicks.

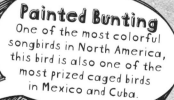

Peach-faced Lovebird
Not only do their facial feathers look like a heart, these birds tend to mate for life.

Painted Bunting
One of the most colorful songbirds in North America, this bird is also one of the most prized caged birds in Mexico and Cuba.

Kiwi

Endangered & Extinct Birds

Quetzal
Many people hunt these birds for their beautiful feathers.

Even though people are working hard to protect birds and other animals, we are still doing things that can hurt them. As a result, some of our world's most amazing creatures have disappeared or are dying out. Many species of birds are endangered, threatened, or extinct.

Bird habitats are being destroyed to build condos, hotels, and other buildings and by overfishing, pollution, pesticides, and water drainage.

If that happens, birds that stay in one place for their whole lives, like the Island Brown Kiwi, have nowhere to live.

The good news is that hard work and dedication can save birds. Bald Eagles used to be endangered. It took a lot of hard work and conservation efforts, and now our nation's bird is only slightly threatened. But there are still many birds in trouble.

Health Hen
The male hen had unusual colorful pouches on his neck and crown that made booming sounds which attracted females.

Black Robin
At one time there were only five of these birds left in New Zealand, but thanks to a Black Robin named Old Blue, another named Old Yellow, and a successful breeding program, five turned into 250!

Brown Pelican

Saving the Gulf!

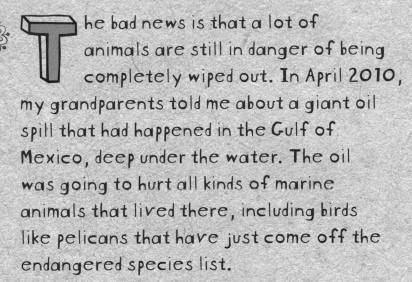

Dear Audubon Society,

As you all are aware of the oil spill in the Gulf is devistating. My mom has already donated a lot of money to help but I have an idea that may also help. I am a decent drawer, and I was wondering if I could sell some bird paintings and give the profits to your orginization. My mom is in town with an art gallery where I live. She is going to sell them these. I also am hoping to go to college in the future. I want to become an ornithouist. I know a few species of birds. I also acknowledge that this is breeding time for plovers, terns, etc. I will do all in my strength to earn money. All I need is your ok.

Here is a pictore of a northern cardinal as a sample.

Thank you for your time.

Olivia
11 years old
and willing to help.

The bad news is that a lot of animals are still in danger of being completely wiped out. In April 2010, my grandparents told me about a giant oil spill that had happened in the Gulf of Mexico, deep under the water. The oil was going to hurt all kinds of marine animals that lived there, including birds like pelicans that have just come off the endangered species list.

I got really upset. My first memory of birds is of the Brown Pelicans and the Great Blue Herons that live in Alabama. My granny and granddad would take me fishing and show me those beautiful birds. Who was going to save them?

I ran right upstairs and wrote a letter to Audubon. I told them that I was willing to help, and I wanted to make a difference for those birds. I wanted to be their voice.

ASPCA's "Kid of the Year" award

Disney's Friends for Change
with Kevin Jonas
© Steve Nesius/Disney Channel

{ A Kiwi! }

Hoda Kotb and
Kathie Lee Gifford

Congressman Steve Israel
and my brother, Jackson

Birding with Audubon's
Woody Wheeler

{ A Puffin! }

{ Olivia with a little bird friend! }

Olivia's
$100G Gift

In the news!

I Love Birds!

Audubon read my letter and said they'd be happy to accept my help. Since I like to draw birds, I decided I would donate bird paintings to people who contributed money to Audubon's Gulf clean-up campaign.

Slowly we spread the word online, and the first donation came in. I was thrilled that someone wanted to help out. My first thought was **I just took a first step for those birds!**

After that, the donations kept pouring in. We got 500 requests for paintings in the first month!

Since starting the **Save the Gulf** campaign, I have spoken in Washington, D.C. on behalf of clean energy. I also visited Project Puffin where I got to hold some tern chicks—and ended up with "endangered poop!" And, I have been able to spread the word about animal preservation at the TEDx conventions, on television, on the radio, and in magazines.

The message I keep telling everyone is that all animals are special and important to our ecosystem. We need to work together to protect them. Imagine if a hundred years from now, children wouldn't get to see the variety of beautiful creatures on this planet. We can't let that happen.

My whole life has been connected to nature, and this is the only Earth we've got. We can't move to another planet, so we have to try to fix Earth. We only have one chance to do it.

If I were President of the United States of America, I would make regulations for fishing companies to limit the amount of fishing. I would stop deforestation and create a Tree Planting Day. Whoever plants the most trees will get a prize. I would encourage people to get together and adopt animals from shelters instead of buying pets from stores.

Also, I would make sure that we all used cleaner energy to preserve our Earth. We need to put the "eco" back in our economy!

Even though I'm not the President, I know I can make a difference—and so can you. Kids CAN do important things to preserve our Earth, such as:

What you can do!

- Build a bird feeder
- Put out unprocessed birdseed or sunflower seeds in your yard to feed birds
- Set up a recycling group in your school or house
- Cut down on paper consumption
- Recycle EVERY DAY
- Compost eggs shells, banana peels, orange peels, and other food garbage. It will turn into dirt that you can use to plant trees.

Make sure to tell everybody what you are doing to save our environment. Spread the word! Kids can definitely make a difference, and I'm here to prove it.

Baltimore Oriole

Common Grackle

Purple Martin

House Finch

Common Nighthawk

Plover

Peregrine Falcon

Organizations:

Throughout my fundraiser, many kids from all over the world have contacted me, looking for ways to help. Some, like me, have made artwork, while others have participated in walkathons. We are the future generation, and even though one person can make a difference, together we can change our planet. Thank you to everyone who is working to help our environment.

Liv.B

National Audubon Society www.audubon.org
National Wildlife Federation www.nwf.org
The Nature Conservancy www.nature.org
Sierra Club www.sierraclub.org
Project Puffin www.projectpuffin.org
Cornell Ornithology Lab www.birds.cornell.edu

About the Author

Olivia Bouler is eleven years old and lives on Long Island with her parents and little brother Jackson. An avid bird lover, aspiring ornithologist, artist, and saxophone player, Olivia spends most vacations visiting her cousins and grandparents in Alabama and Louisiana.

In November 2010, Olivia received the ASPCA's "Tommy P. Monahan" Kid of the Year Award for her commitment and dedication to animal welfare. She currently spends much of her time working on various environmental efforts and attending speaking engagements across the country on behalf of bird and wildlife advocacy.

To date, Olivia has drawn over 120 different species of birds and created over 500 paintings to raise more than $150,000 for her Save the Gulf campaign.